A Moment with God

For:

From:

Bill & Connie

Other books in this series

A Moment with God for Teens

A Moment with God for Teachers

A Moment with God for Sunday School Teachers

A Moment with God
for Those Who Grieve

PRAYERS FOR THOSE WHO GRIEVE

Abingdon Press
Nashville

A Moment with God for Those Who Grieve

PRAYERS FOR THOSE WHO GRIEVE

Copyright © 1999, 2011 by Abingdon Press

This book is printed on acid-free paper.

ISBN 978-1-4267-4153-1

Scripture quotations unless noted otherwise are from the Common English Bible. Copyright © 2011 by the Common English Bible. All rights reserved. Used by permission. (www.CommonEnglishBible.com)

Scripture quotations marked NRSV are from the New Revised Standard Version Bible, copyright 1989 by the Division of Christian Education of the National Council of the Churches of Christ in the United States of America. Used by permission. All rights reserved.

11 12 13 14 15 16 17 18 19 20—10 9 8 7 6 5 4 3 2 1
MANUFACTURED IN MEXICO

CONTENTS

Contents

Contents

The Physical Pain of Grief

The king trembled. He went up to the room over the

gate and cried.

—*2 Samuel 18:33*

*T*ake my hand, Lord. I never imagined that the pain of grief could be so overwhelming. I didn't even know I was capable of such powerful emotions. I get the feeling that the source of my tears is some unexplored cavern, deep within. I've never been in a boxing ring, but I imagine this feeling in my gut, which doubles me over, must be similar to taking a boxer's punch to the stomach. I want to throw up, and I have to remind myself to breathe. I keep thinking, *This can't be happening to me.*

Come, Lord Jesus; take my hand and steady my step. Amen.

Help from an Angel

Then a heavenly angel appeared to him and strengthened him.

—Luke 22:43

*H*eavenly Father, my fear is evident in my shaking hands. If I were a tree, I'm afraid I might just shake myself out of the ground and fall. Secure my roots, O Lord. Send an angel to anoint me with strength, as you did for the weeping, bleeding Jesus. Anchor me as I reach deep to grasp your strength and release my fear. Amen.

Support

"You are the ones who have continued with me in my trials."

—Luke 22:28

God of comfort, free me from thinking I can make it on my own. Give me the courage to receive the offers of those who wish to stand beside me. Forgive me for pushing them away, denying that I have needs. Help me find a circle of friends who will not try to fix me or explain death to me, but will simply be with me, absorbing my pain. Amen.

Four Friends

Some people arrived, and four of them were bringing to him a man who was paralyzed. They couldn't carry him through the crowd, so they tore off part of the roof above where Jesus was. When they had made an opening, they lowered the mat on which the paralyzed man was lying.

—Mark 2:3-4

*M*erciful God, send me four friends who might carry me when I need carrying and listen to me when I need someone to listen. Send me four friends who will pray with me and offer their faith when mine is failing. May their songs rise when mine are silent. Your love through four good friends can deliver me to your healing touch. Amen.

Confusion

While the disciples were behind closed doors . . . Jesus came and stood among them. He said, "Peace be with you."

—*John 20:19*

*A*lmighty Father, I am confused by grief. In a single moment, I first want to be closely held and then I want to be given space to work things out for myself. I have deep feelings of both rage and compassion. Am I going crazy?

O God, speak to me your peace, as you did with your disciples long ago when they were confused and afraid. Give me patience with myself and assure me that time will wash away this confusion. Amen.

Using Anger as a Weapon

Fools show all their anger.

—*Proverbs 29:11*

*D*ear God, I feel like a lightning storm, wildly flashing out of control. My eyes are wild with rage. There is electricity running through my veins.

I'm not comfortable with this anger; when I sense it rising, keep me from using it as a weapon, wounding innocent people. Keep me from focusing the rage inward, torturing myself into depression. Help me develop an anger gauge to monitor and control myself. Amen.

Harnessing the Gift of Anger

When Jesus entered the temple, he threw out those
who were selling things there.

—*Luke 19:45*

*M*y eyes flash fire like yours did, Jesus, when you entered the Temple. Help me see my anger as a gift of energy that can be transformed to create something meaningful. May it fuel me to speak out against injustice and to lift up the weak and forgotten. May it help me create a work of art through words, song, or paint. May it even enable me to help others harness their own anger.

Lord, I don't want to waste this gift on trivial matters; I want to use it to spread your Kingdom. Help me do so in a loving, useful way. Amen.

Faith

The LORD is my shepherd. . . .

He lets me rest in grassy meadows;

he leads me to restful waters;

he keeps me alive.

—Psalm 23:1-3

*L*oving Shepherd, as I walk through dark valleys, give me the patience to simply lie in your green pasture, trusting and waiting to see what gifts you bring me. May a gentle breeze fill my lungs with fresh air and hope. May I drink in your presence from an overflowing cup of living water and feel the healing touch of your oil-anointed hands. Help me trust, Lord, that there is no need to fear anything that comes toward me, because I can trust in you. Surely goodness and mercy shall follow me all the days of my life. Amen.

Questions

My God! My God,

why have you left me all alone?

—Psalm 22:1

*A*lmighty God, like an unpredictable geyser, questions keep shooting into my mind and I shout them to you. Am I being punished? Did I bring this on myself? Why are you so cruel to tease me with love and then take it away like a thief? Are you out there, or am I just playing games? Will my loved one recognize me in heaven?

I am grateful that you can handle my questions. Transform this hot stream of questions into a healing rain to quench my thirsty soul as I grieve my mortality. Amen.

Fishing

Simon Peter told them, "I'm going fishing."

—*John 21:3*

*L*ord Christ, after the crucifixion, the disciples were in the deep water of grief and found comfort in returning to the familiar routine of fishing. I expect that healing came through the everyday toil of casting and pulling nets.

Fill me with the energy and patience to maintain my routine, casting my nets into the deep even when I'm catching no fish. Come to me on the water as you did with Simon Peter. Maybe then I will find the courage to take a leap of faith and walk boldly in new ways. Amen.

May I Tell You?

"I brought you up from Egypt."

—Judges 2:1

O Great Listener, send kind and patient persons with whom I can share my stories. How many times was the story of the exodus told and retold before the people believed in your saving grace? Give me the words to tell the drama and the wisdom to see your saving hand, even in my trials. May each telling make my load lighter, and if I'm really lucky, perhaps on the thousandth time my burden will be as light as a hummingbird.

Thank you, God, for grace-filled friends who can sweep away my pain. Amen.

The Gift of Tears

When Jesus saw her crying . . . he was deeply
disturbed and troubled. . . . Jesus began to cry.
    —John 11:33, 35

*C*ompassionate One, if eyes are windows to the soul, my windows have been stuck on a continuous rinse-cycle. Sometimes the tears won't stop flowing. Yet, to my surprise, at other times my eyes feel dry and cold. I'm pretty hard on myself—I try to stop crying when I cry, and I feel guilty when I can't.

Release me from this endless guilt. May I learn from you, Jesus, that it is okay to weep for myself and my friends. Give me patience, so that your tears and the tears of others will soften my heart to feel once more. Amen.

The Insurance Check

Simon Peter said to Jesus, "Lord, where are you going?"

Jesus answered, "Where I am going, you can't follow me now. . . ."

Peter asked, "Lord, why can't I follow you now?"

—*John 13:36-37*

*H*ere it is, God: a lousy life-insurance check. Of all the ways to measure the worth of a life, this check isn't one of them. I can't bring myself to take it to the bank—it seems so final. To let go too quickly isn't right. How long should I wear black, absorbed in sadness with the insurance check in the drawer?

Give me permission, Lord, to let go without feeling guilty. You'll go with me to the bank, won't you, Lord? Maybe tomorrow. I know your disciples didn't want to let Jesus go, but you gave them permission to keep living. Give me that same grace, Lord. Amen.

Super Ball

Mary stood outside near the tomb, crying. . . . Mary Magdalene

left and announced to the disciples, "I've seen the Lord."

—John 20:11, 18

O God, like a rubber super ball bouncing up and down, my emotions rise and fall. With such extreme highs and lows, I feel as if I am going crazy. Am I losing my mind, or is this all part of mourning?

For just a moment, speak your comforting words to calm my bouncing emotions as you did with Mary Magdalene. I close my eyes and imagine your compassionate voice singing my name, as you did Mary's. One word from you could calm my stormy soul. Amen.

After a Long Illness

My whole being thirsts for you!

My body desires you

    in a dry and tired land,

    no water anywhere.

—*Psalm 63:1*

*H*ealing Spirit, caring for the dying brings surprises. There were times when I laughed as my loved one was out of her mind, saying silly things. At other times we were still and silent, looking deep into each other's moist eyes and simply holding hands. After such a hard illness, I hate to admit it, but death is a relief.

Forgive me for this feeling, and grant me the peace and rest for which I thirst. It is good to know that death is not the end, but a next step. After I regain my strength, help me take *my* next step toward embracing life. Show me the path, dear Lord. Amen.

Comforting Words of Jesus

"Don't be troubled.... My Father's house has room to spare. If that weren't the case, would I have told you that I'm going to prepare a place for you?"

—John 14:1-2

*D*ear Jesus, when your disciples feared the future, you assured them that death is not the end, and that you intended to be together with them in heaven. I can't understand the mystery of death, but I can close my eyes and imagine you compassionately speaking to me: "Don't be troubled." These words bring comfort to my troubled heart. Rekindle the fire of belief in the mysterious world that you have prepared for us. Amen.

Faith and Doubt

Jesus immediately reached out and grabbed him, saying, "You man of weak faith! Why did you begin to have doubts?"

—Matthew 14:31

I confess, God, that I am no better than Peter. One minute I am ready to step out of the boat, taking a leap of faith, and the next minute I question your existence and find myself thrashing the water for air. Surely there must be an element of doubt in faith.

Even in my doubts, Lord Jesus, reach out your hand and hold me up, just as you did Peter. May my doubts and questions not bring panic but lead me to a stronger faith. I will light a candle as an act of faith so that we'll both know I'm serious. May its light lead me to you. Amen.

God, My Rock

I will say to God, my solid rock,

    "Why have you forgotten me?

    Why do I have to walk around,

    sad, oppressed by enemies?"

    —Psalm 42:9

*A*lmighty God, my life is like the psalmist's lament. It is as if I have walked across a swift, shallow mountain stream and stepped into a hole, making a dramatic splash. People laugh at my clumsiness, and I feel dim-witted. Yet even when I perceive that I am cursed and alone, I will hope in you. Don't let my foot slip on this treacherous path. I carefully climb upon you, my rock. Amen.

Confusion about the Resurrection

He was buried, and he rose on the third day.... He appeared to more than five hundred ... and ... he appeared to me.... So if the message that is preached says that Christ has been raised from the dead, then how can some of you say, "There's no resurrection of the dead"?

—1 Corinthians 15:4, 6, 8, 12

*D*ear Jesus, like the Corinthian Christians, I am confused about the resurrection of the dead. Your whole body disappeared, and you could move between earth and heaven and even walk through locked doors. I'm embarrassed to admit it, Jesus, but I wish you would appear to me the way you did to Paul and the others. Yet without a miraculous experience, I join the Corinthian Christians and trust in your resurrection and ours. I will trust the testimonies of the great company of faithful. Grant me this gift of faith, I pray. Amen.

Relationships

Yes, my enemies have been

talking about me;

those who stalk me plot together. . . .

My God, hurry to help me!

—Psalm 71:10, 12b

$\mathcal{L}$ord, the piercing looks of my friends and coworkers tell me that they are annoyed with me and want me to get my life back to normal. But life is not normal! My life can never be like it was! Why can't they understand that? There is a sharp edge to my tongue, and I have no patience with others' concerns. It is hard for me to fret over the things they care about.

God, grant me the grace to soften my attitude. Grant me the patience to hold my tongue when needed, and the wisdom to know when my insights need to be shared. Amen.

Whom Will I Kiss Goodnight?

God is our refuge and strength,

a help always near

in times of great trouble.

—Psalm 46:1

$\mathcal{B}$e present, Lord, for I am lost and empty. There is one fewer place to set at the table. One fewer face to greet in the morning, and one fewer cheek to kiss goodnight. With whom will I eat? Whom will I greet and kiss? The empty void causes a pain in my stomach. I long for arms to reach out and hold me. I long for someone to kiss me goodnight and wake me in the morning.

These are long, dark days, O God, my refuge and strength. Teach me to cope with the pain that echoes through the emptiness in my life. Amen.

A Rainy-Day Plan

Sarah said, "God has given me laughter. Everyone who hears about it will laugh with me."

—Genesis 21:6

$\mathcal{T}$oday, Lord, I will get some fresh flowers for my table. I will wear my brightest comfortable clothes, and dance to loud happy music. Why? Because the cloudy skies threaten to bring me down. On this day I am a soldier, fighting a war against the blues. I'll make cookies, invite friends over, and we will tell our most embarrassing moments and funniest tales. Today, Lord, I will fight my pity party with the gift of joy and laughter. Amen.

Exercise

Jesus asked him, "What do you want me to do for you?"

The blind man said, "Teacher, I want to see."

—Mark 10:51

*O*Giver of Life, I confess that I do want healing, but I've been lazy. Help me care for my body through a regular exercise program. Like Bartimaeus, I must get up and move to receive the healing I seek. When I sit in my self-pity, send someone to give me a kick in the pants, to help me stand, stretch, and walk. Perhaps the next time someone asks, "Can I help you?" I will say, "Yes, you can exercise with me!"

Lord, help me commit to rise up and work out, to assist you with my healing. Amen.

Denial

It scorched him, and he didn't know it;

    it burned him,

        but he didn't give it much thought.

—*Isaiah 42:25b*

Sustaining Spirit, I'm surprised at how well I've handled this death. I've performed like a little soldier without missing a step. I anticipated more sadness, but I haven't really felt anything at all. I hope I can continue to remain in control.

Kind Lord, I wonder why my stomach is in such a knot? I've sure had a lot of heartburn today. Maybe it was something I ate. What did I swallow that is causing such distress? Amen.

Transforming Bitterness: Naomi

She replied to them, "Don't call me Naomi, but call me Mara, for the Almighty has made me very bitter."

—Ruth 1:20

The women said to Naomi, "May the LORD be blessed, who today hasn't left you without a redeemer."

—Ruth 4:14

*A*lmighty God, bitterness is eating away at me the way termites eat a wooden house. My teeth are set on edge, for you have dealt bitterly with me.

Transform my bitterness into thanksgiving, as you did for Naomi. May I be blessed by just one person who shows me kindness, and may that person's love free me. Help me concentrate on the gift I once had rather than on my loss. I can't do it alone, dear Lord. I need your help. Amen.

Another Lost Coin

"Or what woman, if she owns ten silver coins and loses one of them, won't light a lamp and sweep the house, searching her home carefully until she finds it?"

—Luke 15:8

$\mathcal{L}$ord, I keep losing things—gloves at the church, my coat at a friend's, keys at the store, and my glasses . . . somewhere. No one told me grief chipped away your memory.

Give me a light that I may find the things I've lost, and a sense of humor to laugh at myself. Remind me to make a few extra sets of keys and prepare for the inevitable. Amen.

Strength

May the glory be to God who can strengthen you.

—Romans 16:25

*M*ighty God, with one arm, you can lift a constellation. Your power is beyond measure. Could you share just a fraction of your strength with me now? My legs are betraying me, and my will is hiding. Train my leg muscles to carry these heavy burdens. Restore my wandering willpower to push me toward the future. Fortify every vein and blood vessel with fresh oxygen of perseverance. In every cell, plant the seed of hope that a new day will dawn and turn my mourning into dancing. Amen.

A Birthday Prayer

I thank my God every time I mention you in my prayers.

—*Philemon 4*

*H*oly One, on this, my beloved's birthday, I give myself the gift of remembering. I take out the memory box I've made of special items—a comb, photos, letters, videos, and a worn-out wallet. It is a bittersweet gift, and I give myself permission to stop looking at any point without shame. One at a time, I lift sacred items out of the box, close my eyes, and cherish the memory, offering a prayer of thanksgiving. Slowly, I place each item on the table.

Lord, help me celebrate the memories of life, and give me the courage to intentionally create new ones. Amen.

Financial Woes

Save me, God,

   because the waters have reached my neck!

   —Psalm 69:1

*S*ave me, O God, for I'm up to my neck in financial woes. Bearing grief is enough, but the extra burdens of the checkbook, paying bills, and insurance claims are overwhelming.

Why must living and dying be so complicated? Give me a clear mind as I approach this important work. Amen.

Gifts, Not Possessions

You must have no other gods before me.

—Deuteronomy 5:7

*I*t is a hard thing you ask, Lord, that we love nothing more than you—not even our spouse, children, or parents. I confess that I have worshipfully knelt before those I love like an idol I possessed rather than a gift to enjoy. Forgive me, as I relax my grip. I am grateful for the gift I had and will have again. Fill me with peace to love you before all else. Amen.

Do Something Big!

We live by faith and not by sight.

—*2 Corinthians 5:7*

$\mathcal{L}$ead me, Lord, to work out my grief by taking on a project. Maybe I could sew a quilt, putting some of my grief into each stitch and patch. I could give the quilt to someone who is cold, and it would provide comfort and warmth.

Help me be like Noah, who thought big. Help me focus my grief energy to organize my community or the country to right an injustice. Surely there is an artist within, waiting to boldly paint a new day. With you, Lord, anything is possible! Amen.

Christmas

He lifted me out of the pit of death. . . .

He put a new song in my mouth.

—Psalm 40:2-3a

*G*od, give me a new way to celebrate Christmas. The fact that Christmas will not be the same is obvious, but I keep saying it over and over again, driving myself into a state of deep dread. I would rather avoid Christmas altogether; yet it comes.

Pull me out of the desolate pit, O God. Give me a new way to celebrate your coming into the world. I need a new song, or at least distractions. Lead me to create new holiday traditions that might prove to be as memorable as those of the past. Sing to me a new song. I have waited and waited and am ready to be born anew. Amen.

Staying Busy

Brothers and sisters, we urge you to warn those who are
disorderly. Comfort the discouraged.

—1 Thessalonians 5:14

*C*reator God, like a bee hunting for sweet nectar, I have been busy with distractions. Stopping is too painful. Surprisingly, in my grief I have *discovered* sweet nectar, such as a thirst for learning or the joy of new friends. I am grateful for this unexpected gift of grace. Busyness and work bring comfort, like biting a bullet, but they also have their own rewards. May my work glorify you, O Christ. Amen.

Clay Jars

But we have this treasure in clay pots so that the

awesome power belongs to God and doesn't come from us.

—*2 Corinthians 4:7*

Give me the courage and the opportunity, Lord, to allow your healing light to shine through the broken places in my life. How sharing our sufferings brings healing is a mystery. But deep calls to deep, and healing comes from the depths. May I be unashamed to allow your light and love to spill through the cracks of my soul, O God. Amen.

Is Suffering Meaningful?

If you endure steadfastly when you've done good and suffer for it, this is commendable before God. . . . Christ suffered on your behalf. He left you an example so that you might follow in his footsteps.

—1 Peter 2:20-21

Suffering Servant, I am trying to understand the relation between suffering and meaning. Voluntary suffering as modeled by you is meaningful because you gave your life out of a deep love for the world, revealing the nature of God. However, when children suffer as a result of war, accident, or illness, their suffering is not meaningful in itself because it is involuntary suffering. Rather, the meaning we bring out of involuntary suffering comes from the gifts we receive in the process.

Help me sensibly draw meaning out of my suffering. And, if it is my calling, give me the courage to voluntarily suffer for you. Amen.

Tired

I put all my hope in the LORD.

He leaned down to me;

he listened to my cry for help.

—Psalm 40:1

*D*ear God, grief has shattered me. It is exhausting to pick up the pieces and create a new me. I have trouble staying awake and take naps every day. I awake without feeling rested.

Help me wait patiently for renewed strength as I work through the slow, tiring process of grief. Amen.

Fruits of Grief: Strength

Trouble produces endurance.

—Romans 5:3

*O*Divine Teacher, I've always heard that what does not break me will make me stronger. During this dark journey, I doubted I would ever regain strength. But I've exercised my will to live daily, and it has given me a new level of strength and confidence. My heart was broken, but healing has brought a new sense of power that I didn't have before. Help me use this strength to hold my head high as I listen to your call and move into the future. Amen.

Fruits of Grief: Appreciation of Life

Sorrow is better than laughter,

for by sadness of countenance

the heart is made glad.

—Ecclesiastes 7:3 NRSV

*P*atiently, Lord, I went to the shoreline of sorrow. The sea of mourning has left gifts in the sand. My senses are like frost-colored beach glass. Grief has softened the sharp edges, and they now glisten in the sun. I touch the sand that has tempered me, feeling more alive than ever. My senses are keener, and I relish all the smells, tastes, sights, and sounds. I believe I'm living at a deeper level than before. I've reordered my priorities and now spend more energy delighting in the riches I have, rather than dwelling on what I want or what I lost.

Thank you, God, for these gifts. Amen.

Unfinished Business

Restore us, God!

    Make your face shine

        so that we can be saved!

—Psalm 80:3

*E*ver-loving God, help me continue to work on the unfinished business of my relationship. Death came before we could even understand, much less heal, the wounds of hurtful deeds and words. Help me wrestle with these unresolved issues through the night so that by daybreak, I will receive some peace. I don't want to carry the guilt and shame forever. At daybreak, I will place these issues into your forgiving hands. Amen.

Alzheimer's

How long will you forget me, LORD?

> *Forever?*
>
> *How long will you hide your face*
>
> > *from me?*
>
> *How long will I be left to my own wits,*
>
> *agony filling my heart? Daily?*

—Psalm 13:1-2

*M*any times, I joined the psalmist and cried, "How long, Lord? How long must I face the empty eyes and memory? How long before we unlock the mysteries of this disease?" I prayed: "Give me strength, Lord, for I am exhausted." But now that death has come, I wonder how I will spend my days. Help me remember the good days, and find another focus for my love. In Christ's name, I pray. Amen.

Passing Through the Fire

When you pass through the waters,

   I will be with you;

   when through the rivers,

      they won't sweep over you.

When you walk through the fire,

   you won't be scorched

   and flame won't burn you.

   —Isaiah 43:2

*A*lmighty God, the flames of grief have scathed my soul. The flames come from within and without, but you remain at my side, like asbestos armor shielding me from total consumption. Even when I was too exhausted to pray, you never left me. Your tears join mine and fall on inner burning embers. The tears sizzle into steam and rise, lifting the pain. I offer my puffy, charred hand and place it into your pierced one. Your healing touch takes me to a cooler climate. My heart swells with gratitude and hope. Amen.

Calm My Spirit

So they went and woke Jesus, shouting "Master, Master, we're going to drown!" But he got up and gave orders to the wind and the violent waves. The storm died down and it was calm.

—Luke 8:24

*C*reator God, you fill our night sky with bright constellations. You send wind to spread the seeds, and sun and rain to cause them to sprout. You created all the wonders of the earth. There is no doubt that you can restore life to the dying, yet deaths overtake the young and old every day.

I accept the fact that death is part of the natural world and that you often choose not to calm the winds of death that have brought such pain. Now calm my spirit, Lord, that I may know your peace and praise your name once more. Amen.

Child, Get Up!

They were all crying and mourning for her, but Jesus said,

"Don't cry. She isn't dead. She's only sleeping."

—*Luke 8:52*

*J*esus, I love the story of how you raised Jairus's daughter from the dead by saying those words: "Child, get up!" The child's spirit returned; she got up at once, and you wanted her to eat. How I prayed that you would have said those words to my daughter, so that she would come back to me. I confess that I am jealous of Jairus. Why him, and not me?

My consolation is that you did say, "Child, get up," and that my daughter got up, took your hand, and went with you to heaven. I entrust her into your loving care. I trust that she will continue to live with you forever and ever. Amen.

Jonah

"The waters closed in over me;

    the deep surrounded me . . . .

Yet you brought up my life from the Pit,

    O Lord my God."

    —*Jonah 2:5, 6 NRSV*

*L*ike Jonah, O Saving God, I have been swallowed by deep darkness. In the depths, I feared that death would overtake me. As with Jonah, you mysteriously brought me out of the water. I'm grateful for your grace, but I humbly offer another request: Rescue me now a second time from the selfishness and self-centeredness that consume me. May the flowing waters change my heart with the right attitude to live for you, my Savior. Amen.

Self-Forgiveness

"All the prophets testify about him that everyone who believes in him receives forgiveness of sins through his name."

—Acts 10:43

*F*orgiving Father, you have already welcomed me home with open arms many times. Now I simply need to forgive myself. Today, I will go into the bathroom, look into the mirror, and say, "I forgive you." I will forgive myself for not saving my loved one. I will forgive myself for not having the right words to say and for not being there enough. I will let go of my guilt and shame as I look into the mirror, state my name, and say, "I forgive you." Send forth your healing Spirit that the burden may be lifted. Amen.

Facing the Pain

[Jesus] began to feel sad and anxious.

—Matthew 26:37

*J*esus, I know a little of how you felt when you cried in the garden and were so distressed. I, too, have been afraid. Although you had faith in God's providence, you still didn't want to face the pain. I, too, hesitate rather than face the pain.

Grant me the courage, from your example, to turn and face the pain, so that I can experience the resurrection. Amen.

Misguided Friends

When Job's three friends heard about all this disaster that had

happened to him, they came, each one from his home.

—Job 2:11

*D*ear God, at best, my friends have good intentions, but they are not very helpful. They become philosophers and say, "It was meant to be" or "He got what was coming." They become theologians and say, "God needed another angel in heaven." They become psychologists and say, "Find your warrior archetype and start fighting."

Relieve me from the philosophers, theologians, and psychologists. Send me a friend who will simply hold my hand and help with the dishes. Amen.

Bad News / Good News

We are experiencing all kinds of trouble, but we aren't crushed. We are confused, but we aren't depressed. We are harassed, but we aren't abandoned. We are knocked down, but we aren't knocked out.

    —*2 Corinthians 4:8-9*

*M*ighty God, my afflictions have partially buried me in the sand. But I refuse to be buried. I fight to emerge, stand, and shout, "Hey, I am still here!" The afflictions have not crushed me. I've been confused, but I've kept the faith. I've been ridiculed, but you stayed with me. I've been wounded, but I kept going.

May the good news of enduring and fighting give me the power to keep taking the next step. Amen.

Selling the Farm

Alongside Babylon's streams,

there we sat down,

crying because we remembered Zion.

—Psalm 137:1

*L*ord, the auctioneer's voice sings loudly as I watch my land, house, and belongings sold to the highest bidder, seeing our lives broken apart. With full eyes, I remember a room filled with family, and toddlers pulling themselves up on the table. I imagine echoes of voices in the wind.

Teach me to sing a new song in a strange land. Help me hold my memories as I let go of the possessions. Amen.

Movement Out of Grief

"No one has greater love than to give up one's life for one's friends."

—John 15:13

$\mathcal{L}$oving God, the last movement to heal a broken heart may be the hardest. For months or years, my grief work has consumed me. I have cared for myself, pampered myself, and made myself the number one priority. It's so easy to remain self-consumed, yet one measure of healing is how well we move from self-obsession to thinking of others.

Help me each day make myself available for others and spend energy serving them. I want to live unselfishly, as you have asked. Amen.

O Absalom, My Son, My Son!

"Oh, my son Absalom! Oh, my son! My son Absalom! If only I had died instead of you!"

—2 Samuel 18:33b

*B*lessed One, King David's lament for his son Absalom is so moving. I share David's pain, but I'm afraid to let it out so freely. It's scary to open up your soul. What if the tears flow for an hour or a week? Give me the courage to free my tears so that I will be whole.

Thank you, God, for loving so much that you feel my pain and shed tears for me, even when I cannot do these things for myself. Amen.

The Meaning of Life

Perfectly pointless, says the Teacher,

perfectly pointless. . . .

What do people gain

from all the hard work . . . ?

—Ecclesiastes 1:2-3

You can't understand the work of God, who makes

everything happen.

—Ecclesiastes 11:5

*L*ord, there is an angry person storming around inside me, asking, "What use is there in loving, when those you love never wake from their sleep?" I tried to bind this angry person and gag the questions, until I realized that this person was the same one who believes in you.

It's a lover's quarrel, God. Like the teacher in Ecclesiastes, my questions come from the same deep place as my faith. These questions remind me of my deep connection as I struggle to make sense of mortality. Amen.

Starting the Journey

Jonah got up—to flee.

—Jonah 1:3a

$\mathcal{D}$ear God, did I tell you that I was just fine? I've told everyone I was fine. Lying is acceptable in times like this, isn't it, Lord? I figure if I keep acting fine, then soon I will be fine. If I act as though nothing really terrible happened, then we can all pretend it didn't. It would be selfish to bother others with the unpleasant burden of grief. Surely, Lord, there is an easier path to wholeness than taking off the mask.

Okay, Lord, I'll find a safe place, and tomorrow I will take the mask off for a whole minute. I'll start tomorrow and begin a daily ritual. Tomorrow, Lord, I'll start the journey. Amen.

Ruth

Then she kissed them, and they lifted up their voices and wept. But they replied to her, "No, instead we will return with you, to your people."

—Ruth 1:9b-10

*E*ver-loving God, friends and family who support the grieving are a priceless gift. May I have the same love and charity in my heart for those I love as Ruth had for her mother-in-law, Naomi. Like them, may I find the courage to move from the past to a new place. Bestow upon me Naomi's wisdom to secure stability and new life for my family. These things I pray in the name of Jesus who descended from Ruth. Amen.

Leaning Toward the Pain

By his wounds we are healed.

—Isaiah 53:5b

*S*ecure my feet, Lord, so that I may lean over the edge of the well of pain without falling. Make my back straight, that I can hold my face up and endure the strong, bitter winds. Open the eyes of my heart and head to see the path of healing. Nimble my fingers and stretch my arms that I may touch the wounds and reach deep inside the festering boils. You showed us, Lord, that by facing the worst thing imaginable, we might find new life. Give me the courage to embrace the wounds—including yours, O Christ—that I may know your healing touch. Amen.

Physical Grief

Then he went a short distance farther and fell on his

face and prayed.

—*Matthew 26:39*

*J*esus, in your anguish, you threw yourself on the ground and prayed. You experienced grief with your whole body. I am so self-conscious, I can't imagine letting my whole body grieve. Give me the courage, Lord, to let my grief go so that it will pass through me. Then raise me up from my desperate agony with renewed strength and power. This miracle could only come from you, my comforter, my strength. Amen.

Thanksgiving

Though the fig tree doesn't bloom,

   and there's no produce on the vine;

though the olive crop withers,

   and the fields don't provide food;

though the sheep is cut off

   from the pen,

      and there is no cattle in the stalls;

I will rejoice in the LORD.

   —Habakkuk 3:17-18a

*G*od, you save me and uphold me, even when everything seems to go wrong. To you I cling for my salvation. You alone can fill my emptiness. You alone can bring healing, even if that healing must come at death. My list of complaints is long. I cry out from my depths, and you alone offer the water to quench my true thirst. So on this day, I raise my voice in praise and thanksgiving, hoping only in God. Amen!

Time

But those who hope in the Lord

will renew their strength;

they will fly up on wings like eagles;

they will run and not be tired;

they will walk and not be weary.

—Isaiah 40:31

*T*hey say that time brings healing, Lord, and I know it is true. It takes time to reconstruct a life. Knowing that in time I, too, will run and not be weary, walk and not faint, gives me hope.

When I am impatient, remind me, Lord, that muscles don't grow overnight, but only after daily exercise. Amen.

Nothing Can Separate

Who will separate us from Christ's love? Will we be separated by trouble, or distress, or harassment, or famine, or nakedness, or danger, or sword?

—Romans 8:35

Empower me, God, to stand tall under hardship. With you on my side, there is nothing I cannot conquer. With you on my side, who can be against me? I want to stay close to you, Lord, so that we will endure this together. Amen.